PRIMARY SOURCES OF
FAMOUS PEOPLE IN AMERICAN HISTORY™

DAVY CROCKETT

FRONTIER HERO

J. T. MORIARTY

rosen central
Primary Source™
The Rosen Publishing Group, Inc., New York

Published in 2004 by The Rosen Publishing Group, Inc.
29 East 21st Street, New York, NY 10010

First Edition

Library of Congress Cataloging-in-Publication Data
Moriarty, J.T.
Davy Crockett: frontier hero / J.T. Moriarty. — 1st ed.
      p. cm. — (Primary sources of famous people in American history)
Summary: Surveys the life of the American frontiersman who became a member of
Congress and died trying to defend the Alamo.
Includes bibliographical references (p.   ) and index.
ISBN 0-8239-4108-6 (lib. bdg.)
ISBN 0-8239-4180-9 (pbk.)
6-pack ISBN 0-8239-4307-0
1. Crockett, Davy, 1786–1836—Juvenile literature. 2. Pioneers—Tennessee—Biography—
Juvenile literature. 3. Frontier and pioneer life—Tennessee—Juvenile literature. 4. Tennessee—
Biography—Juvenile literature. 5. Legislators—United States—Biography—Juvenile literature.
6. United States. Congress. House—Biography—Juvenile literature. 7. Alamo (San Antonio,
Tex.)—Siege, 1836—Juvenile literature. [1. Crockett, Davy, 1786–1836. 2. Pioneers. 3.
Legislators.] I. Title. II. Series.
F436.C95M66 2003
976.8'04'092—dc21
                                                                        2003003808

Manufactured in the United States of America

Photo credits: cover © Burstein Collection/Corbis; p. 5 Tennessee Historical Society; pp. 6, 13 (bottom), 20 Lawrence County Archives, Lawrenceburg, Tennessee; p. 7 Library of Congress Prints and Photographs Division, HABS, TENN, 47-KNOVI, 4-2; pp. 8, 25 Library of Congress Geography and Map Division; p. 9 Jefferson County Archives, Dandridge, Tennessee; p. 10 David Crockett's Rifle, Gift of Mr. and Mrs. Paul L. Failor, the Alamo Collection, photograph courtesy of the Daughters of the Republic of Texas Library; pp. 11, 15 Texas State Capital, Austin, Texas; pp. 13 (top) (No. 92-128), 27 (No. 75-556) The Institute of Texan Cultures; p. 16 courtesy of the St. Louis Art Museum; p. 17 Tennessee State Library and Archives, Archives and Manuscript Collections; p. 19 National Portrait Gallery, Smithsonian Institution/Art Resource, NY; p. 21 The Beinecke Rare Book and Manuscript Library, Yale University Library; p. 23 The Phelps Stokes Collection, Miriam and Ira D. Wallach Division of Art, Prints and Photographs, the New York Public Library, Astor, Lenox, and Tilden Foundations; p. 24 Independence National Historical Park; p. 26 Center for American History, University of Texas at Austin; p. 28 Maura Boruchow; p. 29 © Corbis.

Designer: Thomas Forget; Editor: Jill Jarnow; Photo Researcher: Rebecca Anguin-Cohen

CONTENTS

1 DAVY'S EARLY YEARS

Tennessee was a wilderness in 1786. That's the year Davy Crockett was born. There were woods, fields, and lots of wild animals. There were dirt roads and a few small farms. People were poor.

Davy's father owned a tavern. He owed money to a lot of people. Davy couldn't go to school. He worked to help support his family.

DID YOU KNOW?

When Davy was born, Tennessee was part of North Carolina. It didn't become a state until 1796. Davy was 10.

Davy Crockett was born in this small wooden house in 1786.
The house, near Rogersville, Tennessee, is now a historic site.

When they could afford it, Davy's parents forced him to go to school. Davy didn't like that. He ran away from home. He lived in Virginia. While he was away, he worked at many jobs. After two years, Davy returned home. He was very sorry for having left.

Davy worked to help his father pay his debts. His boss was a man named Mr. Kennedy.

Davy's father owned a gristmill business, where he would grind grain. Everything washed away in a flood. The gristmill pictured here was built to look like his.

The Chisholm Tavern *(above)* was built in 1792 in Knox County, Tennessee. The Crockett family tavern may have looked a lot like this one.

Davy finally decided he wanted to learn to read. Most farmers couldn't read. Davy thought reading would make him special. He went to a school that was run by Mr. Kennedy's son. Later Davy said he learned to read in six months.

On his 20th birthday, Davy married Polly Finley. They had a farm in the wilderness.

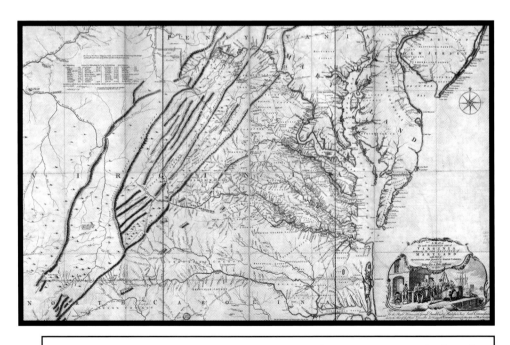

This map shows the parts of Virginia where most people lived in 1775. Davy Crockett worked in Virginia for two years.

Know all men by these presents that we David Crockett and Thomas Doggett are held and firmly bound unto John Sevier Governor and his successors in office in the sum of Twelve hundred & fifty Dollars to be void on condition there be no cause to obstruct the marriage of the said David Crockett with Polly Findley. Witness our hands and seals this 12th day of August 1806

Test
J. Hamelton

David Crock [seal]
Thos Doggett [seal]

Davy Crockett and Polly Finley were married on August 12, 1806. This is their marriage license.

The Creek War was part of the War of 1812. England and Spain convinced the Creek Indians to kill American settlers. They supplied the Creeks with guns and ammunition.

Davy joined the fight. He served under General Andrew Jackson. The settlers won the war. Jackson became a hero.

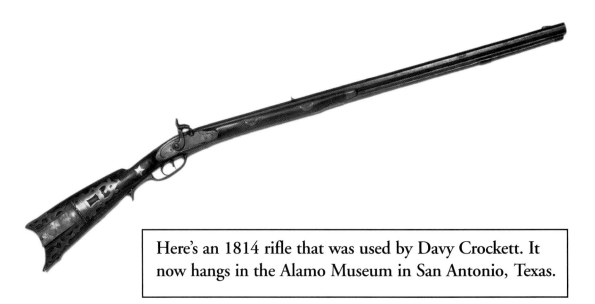

Here's an 1814 rifle that was used by Davy Crockett. It now hangs in the Alamo Museum in San Antonio, Texas.

In this painting, Davy Crockett wears a buckskin suit. In one hand he holds a coonskin cap. He also holds his rifle, which he called Betsy.

2 DAVY THE FRONTIERSMAN

Davy and Polly's sons were named John and William. Their daughter was named Margaret. Polly got very sick and died. Davy was very sad. But he married again. His new wife was named Elizabeth.

Davy became a famous bear hunter. His family ate the meat he brought home. He said he had killed 105 bears in a single season.

SHOOTING IN THE DARK

Davy was a sharpshooter. He won many contests. Sometimes he and his friends shot at candles in the dark. They tried to blow them out with the wind of the bullets.

COLONEL DAVID CROCKETT.

Davy was sometimes called Colonel David Crockett. Left is a dried gourd he used to store gunpowder. It was made before 1822.

Davy tried many jobs. He had bad luck. Like his father, Davy owned a mill that washed away in a flood. He also tried to sell wood. He chopped down trees with his friends. They started to float them down the Mississippi River. The river was too strong. Their boats sank near Memphis. Davy nearly drowned.

DID YOU KNOW?

Davy Crockett was elected colonel of the fifty-seventh militia regiment of Lawrence County, Tennessee, in 1818.

This portrait shows what Davy looked like when he served in the U.S. Congress.

They were rescued by some men from Memphis. Davy became friends with some of these men. They are the people who helped him start his career in politics.

Davy liked to tell stories about the days he worked on the river. This famous painting by George Caleb Bingham shows what life on the river looked like.

Tennessee leaders sent this constitution to
Philadelphia when they applied for statehood.
Tennessee became a state in 1796.

3 DAVY GOES TO WASHINGTON

Davy had a colorful personality. He was good with people. When he spoke, he told funny stories. Audiences enjoyed them. People respected and trusted him. They felt that Davy was like them.

THE REAL DEAL

Someone wrote a book about Davy. Davy said a lot of it was untrue. It made him mad. So, he wrote his own book about himself.

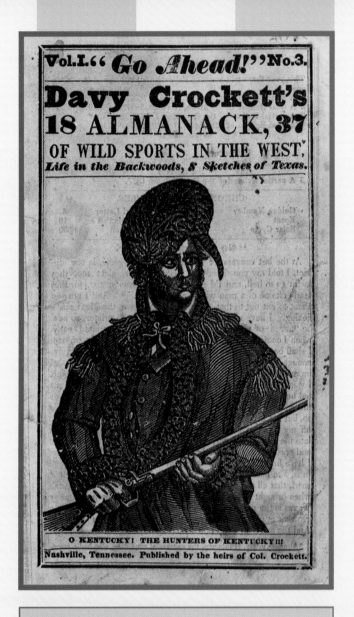

Vol. I. "*Go Ahead!*" No. 3.

Davy Crockett's
18 ALMANACK, 37
OF WILD SPORTS IN THE WEST,
Life in the Backwoods, & Sketches of Texas.

O KENTUCKY! THE HUNTERS OF KENTUCKY !!!

Nashville, Tennessee. Published by the heirs of Col. Crockett.

Almanacs about the adventures of Davy Crockett were published from 1835 to 1856. They usually had "Go Ahead!" printed on the cover. This was part of Davy's famous motto.

Davy became a living legend. People wrote books and stories about him. Someone wrote a play. Davy liked the attention. He had a famous motto: "Be always sure you're right, then go ahead."

He was elected to local public offices. Davy ran for state legislature in 1821. He won. Each office he held was more important than the last.

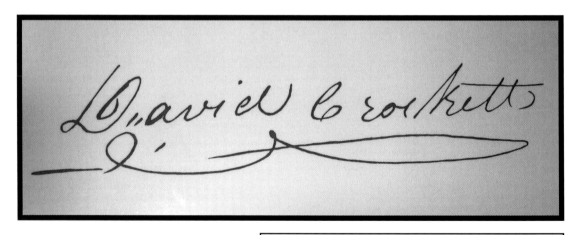

In 1817, Davy was elected justice of the peace in Lawrence County, Tennessee. This is his signature from a contract he signed in 1820.

Vol. 2.]   "GO AHEAD!!"   [No. 3.

THE CROCKETT ALMANAC
1841.

Tussel with a Bear. See page 9.

**Containing Adventures, Exploits, Sprees
& Scrapes in the West, &
Life and Manners in the Backwoods.**

Nashville, Tennessee. Published by Ben Harding.

Davy's legend grew thanks to Davy Crockett almanacs. Filled with tall tales about hunting in the wilderness, they continued to be published for 20 years after Davy died.

Davy was elected to the United States Congress in 1827. He was reelected in 1833. He was a good congressman. He voted to help his people. They were farmers and frontiersmen. He tried to protect the Indians, too. Davy didn't like it when laws only helped the rich.

WHAT'S IN A NAME?

Davy's nickname in Congress was the Gentleman from the Cane. Cane is a kind of rough grass. The nickname made fun of him. It meant Davy was from the woods. But Davy turned the tables by laughing at it.

Davy worked hard in Washington as a congressman from Tennessee. This 1832 painting shows the hall where Congress members argued about ideas and laws.

4 REMEMBER THE ALAMO

General Andrew Jackson had become president of the United States. Davy disagreed with President Jackson's ideas. He spoke out in Congress. The president got mad. This caused trouble.

Davy was not reelected to Congress in 1835. He lost by 250 votes. At first, Davy was sad. Then he decided to move to Texas.

Davy wanted the government to let the Indians stay on their own land. President Jackson *(pictured left)* did not agree. He and Davy became enemies.

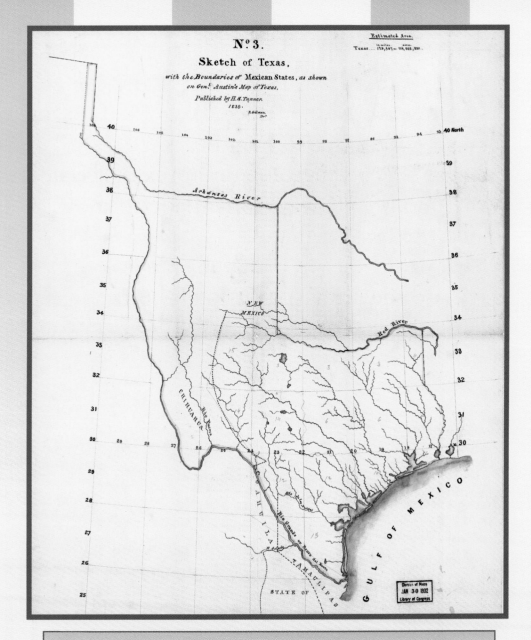

The boundaries of Texas can be seen on this early map.
Davy wanted to be part of the new government of Texas.

In 1836, Texas wasn't yet part of the United States. It was part of Mexico. Davy liked Texas. It was a good place to hunt bears.

There was a war going on in Texas. People wanted to break away from Mexico. Davy joined the Texas army.

The Alamo was an old Spanish mission. Davy and the army got trapped there.

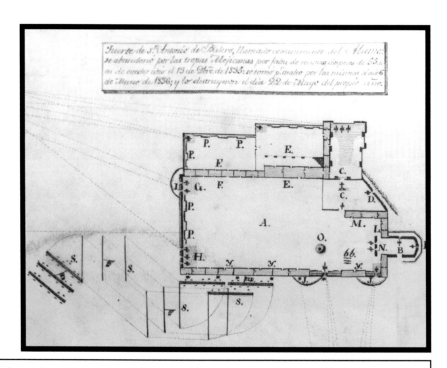

The Alamo was built in 1718 as a mission to teach Christianity to Indians. Abandoned by 1836, the Alamo became the "cradle of Texas Liberty."

Davy and 188 other Texans held off General Santa Anna and his large Mexican army from inside the Alamo. In the end, the Mexican army killed all the Texans, including Davy.

The Mexican army attacked. They killed Davy and everyone else. No one was left alive.

Davy died, but his legend continued. "Remember the Alamo!" people said. It was a battle cry. Eventually, the Texas army won. Texas became a state. People still remember Davy Crockett and his heroic life.

A marble monument stands at the Alamo. It celebrates those who died fighting for the freedom of Texas. At the center is a statue of Davy Crockett. He was a colorful, hardworking man of the American frontier.

Fall of the Alamo---Death of Crockett.

Davy Crockett is pictured as he is killed in battle. The artist used his imagination to draw Davy's last fight. Davy was 49 years old when he died.

TIMELINE

1786—Davy Crockett is born on August 17.

1806—Davy marries Polly Finley.

1815—Polly dies.

1816—Davy marries Elizabeth Patton.

1821—Davy is elected to the Tennessee Legislature.

1827—Davy is elected to Congress.

1833—Davy is reelected.

1834—Davy publishes his autobiography.

1835—Davy loses bid for reelection. He moves to Texas.

1836—Davy dies in the Battle of the Alamo.

GLOSSARY

Congress (KON-gres) The part of the U.S. government that makes laws. The members of Congress are chosen by the people of each state.

debt (DET) Something owed.

elected (ee-LEK-tid) Chosen for an office by voters.

frontier (frun-TEER) The edge of a settled country, where the wilderness begins.

legislature (LEH-jis-lay-chur) A body of people that has the power to make or pass laws.

living legend (LIHV-ing LEH-jend) A living person about whom there are many stories.

nickname (NIK-naym) A name that is used instead of or in addition to a person's real name.

personality (per-sun-A-lih-tee) A person's behavioral and emotional qualities

public office (PUH-blik AW-fiss) An elected position in which a person helps make laws.

settlers (SET-lerz) People who move to a new land to live.

territory (TER-uh-tor-ee) Land that is controlled by a person or a group of people. In the United States, a territory is an area that is not yet a state.

WEB SITES

Due to the changing nature of Internet links, the Rosen Publishing Group, Inc., has developed an online list of Web sites related to the subject of this book. This site is updated regularly. Please use this link to access the list:

http://www.rosenlinks.com/fpah/dcro

PRIMARY SOURCE IMAGE LIST

Page 5: Davy Crockett birthplace near present-day Rogersville, Tennessee. It is preserved as a historic site by the State of Tennessee Department of Environment and Conservation.

Page 8: Map drawn by Joshua Fry and Peter Jefferson showing parts of Virginia, Maryland, Pennsylvania, New Jersey and North Carolina, 1775.

Page 9: Marriage license of David Crockett and Polly Finley, dated August 12, 1806, Jefferson County Archives, Dandridge, Tennessee.

Page 11: Full-length portrait of David Crockett by William H. Huddle, Texas State Capitol, Austin, Texas.

Page 13: (top) Engraved bust portrait of Colonel David Crockett by J. W. Orr from a drawing by S. Wallin, the American Portrait Gallery, A. D. Jones, J. M. Emerson & Co., New York, 1860; (bottom) gunpowder gourd used by Davy Crockett, given to Thomas Mitchell before 1822.

Page 17: Constitution of Tennessee, 1796, Tennessee State Library and Archives, Archives and Manuscript Collections.
Page 19: Cover, *Davy Crockett's Almanack of Wild Sports in the West*, 1837, National Portrait Gallery, Smithsonian Institution/Art Resource, New York.
Page 20: David Crockett signature, 1820, Lawrence County Archives, Lawrence County, Tennessee.
Page 21: Cover, *The Crockett Almanac*, 1841, Published by Ben Harding, Nashville, TN.
Page 23: The Hall of Representatives, Washington, DC, watercolor by Alexander Jackson Davis, 1832, the Phelps Stokes Collection, Miriam and Ira D. Wallach Division of Art, Prints and Photographs, New York Public Library, Astor, Lennox, and Tilden Foundations.
Page 25: *Sketch of Texas with the Boundaries of Mexican States*, as shown on General Stephen F. Austin's Map of Texas, published by R. S. Tanner, 1839, Library of Congress, Geography and Map Division, Washington, DC.
Page 26: Plan of the Alamo, engraving, Sanchez-Navarro (Jose Juan) Papers, 1831-1839, Center for American History, UT-Austin, Texas.
Page 27: *Storming of the Alamo*, engraving, D. W. C. Baker, *A Texas Scrapbook*, A. S. Barnes & Co., 1875, New York.
Page 29: "Fall of the Alamo—Death of Crockett," from *Davy Crockett's Almanack of Wild Sports in the West,* 1837, Texas Collection Library, Corbis.

INDEX

ABOUT THE AUTHOR

J. T. Moriarty graduated from Oberlin College where he studied art history and wrote criticism for the *Oberlin Review*. He now lives in New York, with two cats, a turtle, and a marmot.